# A View of Bronzeville

by
## Bernard C. Turner

HIGHLIGHTS OF CHICAGO PRESS

# A View
# of Bronzeville

HIGHLIGHTS OF CHICAGO PRESS

DESIGN: CHANDLER/WHITE PUBLISHING COMPANY

CHICAGO, IL

ISBN: 0-9710487-0-3
Library of Congress Control Number: 2001131916
© 2002 HIGHLIGHTS OF CHICAGO PRESS

# A View of Bronzeville

## Introduction/Acknowledgements

Reflecting on my youth in Chicago, I can remember my first home, which was on the corner of Bowen Avenue and Cottage Grove Avenue. My father owned and ran a Standard Oil Station on the opposite side of the street just next to the elevated train tracks. This was the Kenwood Line, which ran a short distance from 43rd and Lake Park to the convergence of several elevated train lines at 38th and Indiana. We lived in a makeshift apartment, one of many in the neighborhood of walkups and tenements, over a business called the Safety Vulcanizing Company at 4145 S. Cottage Grove. Next door was the A.A. Rayner Funeral Home, a strong African-American business in those days and today. Other businesses in the neighborhood included the obligatory tavern, Sago's, where everyone hung out, the grocery stores, the important TV Repair Shop and record store owned by Bob Ellis, the hotel for transients, the cleaners, the first Walgreen's, and the greasy spoon restaurant under the el tracks. This was the Bronzeville of my youth, a neighborhood where people lived and worked and strived to make it. Interestingly enough, it was the only place for people like us to live. We had no idea at the time. It was where we were and where we wanted to live.

This book is dedicated to my parents, Milton A. Turner, Sr. and my mother, Cora Turner, who worked hard and provided for their family as did many in a city of challenge for those of color, for those who migrated north in search of opportunity. I would like to also express thanks to my big brother, Milton A. Turner, Jr., who taught me much and provides me with some of these memories.

I would like to give a special thank you to Sherry Williams, founder of the Bronzeville Historical Society, for her inspiration and dedication to the preservation of the history and culture of African Americans who live in or have lived in Chicago. We began working on the committee of the Mississippi Project with Ramón Price, the late curator of the DuSable Museum of African-American History, Theresa Christopher, Doris Davis, and Oyekunle Oyegbemi, who began and continues this important project today.

To the Chicago Historical Society for its collections and research database and for all of the knowledge I have acquired from the seminars I have attended on Chicago and American History, and from my fellow volunteer interpreters, who give tours of the CHS galleries and neighborhoods.

To all of my friends and colleagues who have given me encouragement to continue to learn and to share my thoughts and deeds.

Bernard C. Turner, President
Bronzeville Historical Society

# A View of Bronzeville

## Table of Contents

# Overview

## Where is Bronzeville?

C hicago has always been a city with neighborhoods—neighborhoods of character, complexion, and color. Neighborhoods in Chicago evolved as the people and groups who inhabited them came and left. The neighborhood you are going to visit became known as Bronzeville, because it was the center of African-American life and culture. Originally known as Douglas/Grand Boulevard (still officially called that), Bronzeville is bounded by 26th Street on the north, 51st Street on the south, Lake Michigan on the east, and the Chicago, Rock Island, and Pacific Railroad tracks on the west.

## What groups of Chicagoans lived in Bronzeville?

C hicago was a crossing point from the East to the Great Lakes to the river routes west and south to the Gulf of Mexico. Native Americans used a trail that cut across the Bronzeville area. This trail became an important commercial route to and from the center of Chicago, and was later named Vincennes Avenue. In the 1850s the area was settled by Irish-Catholic immigrants, who worked at the Illinois Central Railroad car shops nearby. Later, Stephen A. Douglas, Illinois senator and presidential candidate, developed a housing tract for more affluent residents. Douglas' own home, Oakenwald, was built in the vicinity of Cottage Grove and 35th St. Wealthy businessmen also built stately homes in the neighborhood and after the Great Fire of 1871, German Jews relocated to the area.

## The Historic District

During the 1880s and into the new century many frame cottages, as well as elegant residences, were built in the community. The architectural styles varied from Gothic to Romanesque to Queen Anne. Romanesque homes are characterized by rock-faced exterior-wall surfaces with simple door and window treatments. In general, red pressed brick facades, with bay windows and irregular rooflines typify the Queen Anne houses. Many of the residences were designed by leading architects of the time who came to Chicago after the Great Fire of 1871. There are still some homes left in the community, however many of the homes have deteriorated from neglect, due to the unfortunate economic plight of the residents during the Depression and later.

## The Great Migration

More and more African Americans came to Chicago at the end of the nineteenth century and settled in Douglas/Grand Boulevard. They worked as domestics in the homes of the wealthy and provided menial services to businesses in the Loop. The population of African Americans grew dramatically from 85,000 in 1900 to 387,000 in 1940. During World War I, many African Americans came to Chicago from the South, and found jobs in the stockyards and other industries because of labor shortages. The Chicago Defender, one of several African-American newspapers in Chicago at the time, led the call for Blacks to migrate north to escape poverty and racism. Because of the large influx of African Americans to the neighborhood, increasing racial tension erupted in the Race Riots of 1919. As a result, most of the Irish and Jewish residents left the neighborhood. Many of the surrounding neighborhoods began a practice of organizing for the purpose of keeping Blacks from moving out of Bronzeville into their

neighborhoods. This practice of restrictive covenants continued for many years until the landmark 1948 Shelley vs. Kramer
Supreme Court decision outlawed them.

**Chalk writing on railroad cars bound for Chicago:**

> *"Farewell, We're Good and Gone*
> *Bound for the Promised Land"*

**Quote:**

> *"I never see a city that big. All those tall buildings. I thought*
> *they were universities."*
> *Louis Armstrong arriving in Chicago in 1922*

## Bronzeville Blossoms

Besides the laborers, Bronzeville residents included
entrepreneurs, doctors, lawyers, large and small business owners, clerks, and skilled workers educated at
the Freeman Schools of the South. These schools are currently called the Traditionally Black Colleges and Universities.
Bronzeville had theaters for orchestras, vaudeville troupes,
and musical stars like Lena Horne, Nat King Cole, Ray Nance,
Oscar Brown Jr., Louis Armstrong, and Earl "Fatha" Hines.
Indeed, like Harlem in New York, Chicago's Bronzeville experienced what was referred to as a renaissance during the 30s
and 40s in the arts, including dance, photography, and litera-
ture. Talented dancers included Kathryn Dunham and Talley
Beatty; writers Richard Wright, Frank Yerby, Margaret Walker,
Willard Motley, and John H. Johnson (publisher of Ebony);
Pulitzer Prize winning poet, Gwendolyn Brooks; and artists
Elizabeth Catlett, Margaret Burroughs, William Carter, and
Archibald Motley.

Bronzeville was the home of several important cultural and
historical institutions, not the least of which was the 3,000-seat

Regal Theater, the most celebrated of all the clubs, dance halls and theaters to be found in the neighborhood. The Regal was the Mecca for Black drama, music, comedy and cinema, and provided a forum for all the rising entertainers of the time. The theater opened in 1928 as part of a comprehensive commercial real estate development project that included South Center department store and the legendary Savoy Ballroom. In addition to hosting the best in entertainment, the Regal theater also contributed to the cultural and political development of Bronzeville by hosting parties and special events such as the Bud Billiken Club, a children's organization sponsored by Robert Abbott, editor of the Chicago Defender. The depression years brought on a period when people could not afford to go out and the Regal declined in popularity. The Regal Theater was demolished in 1973.

**Quote from "Bronzeville" by St. Clair Drake and Horace Cayton Holiday, 1947**

# *"Chicago's huge Negro community is variously intent upon Staying Alive, Getting Ahead, Praising the Lord, Having a Good Time, and Advancing the Race."*

# The Gap

## *Sites in Bronzeville*

***Bronzeville Sign***
*35th and King Dr.*

***Chess Records*** *Established in 1950*
*2120 South Michigan Ave*

Chess Records was founded by Leonard and Phil Chess, who came to Chicago along with many European Jews seeking a better life in the United States. Theirs is an interesting tale of immigrant success mixed with Black musicians, pioneers in a musical art form born in the south. The Chess brothers worked with artists such as Chuck Berry, Etta James, Bo Diddley, Willie Dixon, and Muddy Waters. Others included Fontella Bass, Ahmad Jamal, and Ramsey Lewis.

Originally an owner of a junkyard, Leonard bought a liquor store, where he opened a soon-to-be popular lounge called the Macoumba. There amid the live performances an idea was formed to start a record business. Leonard has been described as a vulgar, driven man, who immersed himself in the culture of the blues, R & B, and Jazz performers he produced. Many stories have been told about some of the deals that were made with the artists and how Chess Records was involved in some of the payola scandals of the 50's and 60's. However scandalous, success brought much notoriety to the record label and makes it a Bronzeville and Chicago landmark.

*Quinn Chapel AME* is the oldest Black Church in Chicago
2401 S. Wabash

Originally formed as a nondenominational bible study and prayer group in 1844, this congregation met in the home of one of its members. The church became African-American Episcopal in 1847 and was very active in the abolitionist movement in Chicago. Quinn's pastors placed great emphasis on civic and political matters and brought in notable African American and white leaders to speak to the Sunday Forum. After the Great Chicago Fire destroyed the original church in 1871, the congregation moved around until they purchased the present site in 1890. As early as 1902 the church broadened its mission to provide services to its parishioners and the community, including a kindergarten, a savings bank, a library, and an employment bureau. Quinn Chapel continues to be one of the most viable religious institutions in the city.

Quinn Chapel has had more than its share of notable speakers and performers. Two American presidents, Taft and McKinley, have addressed the congregation along with civil rights leaders, Booker T. Washington, Ida B. Wells, and Martin Luther King, Jr. The church has been the set for Oprah Winfrey's movie, *There Are No Children Here*, and Halle Berry's *Losing Isiah*. Recently, Winton Marsalis presented his sacred mass, *In This House, On This Morning*.

*Chicago Daily Defender*—
*The Oldest African-American Newspaper in Chicago*
*2400 S. Michigan*

Founded in 1905 by Robert S. Abbott, this leading African-American newspaper was run by John H. Sengstacke until his death in 1997. Always a champion for the rights of all citizens, the Defender gained influence and was one of first African-American newspapers to reach a circulation of more than 100,000. The newspaper was also instrumental in convincing thousands of African Americans to leave the racial oppression of the South to come north in search of equality, education, employment, and a better life. Abbott designated May 15, 1917 as "The Great Northern Drive" day spurring the Great Migration to Chicago and other cities in the North.

*Chester Commodore cartoon*
*Commemorating the 96th anniversary of the Chicago Defender*

The Defender was also the first to print photos in a three-color process and to issue a full page of comics. Initially a weekly, Sengstacke converted the newspaper into a daily in 1956. Other Sengstacke newspapers were founded subsequently, including the Michigan Chronicle in Detroit in 1936, the Pittsburgh Courier in 1908, and the Tri-State Defender organized in 1951 by John H. Sengstacke to meet the needs of the African-American population near Memphis, including communities in Arkansas, Mississippi, and Tennessee.

The Chicago Daily Defender was housed in a former Jewish synagogue at 34th and Indiana. This site was designated a national landmark in 1998. The Defender's current site is this historic building opened in 1956

***Ada S. McKinley Educational Services***
*100 E. 34th Street, Silas Purnell, Director*

A division of Ada S. McKinley Community Services, Inc., Ada S. McKinley Educational Services provides assistance to students seeking admission to colleges and universities, including educational preparation and placement. Founded in 1918 by an African-American teacher who emigrated from Texas, the foundation has become one of the oldest and most successful social service agencies in Chicago. The services include childcare, mental health care, foster care and adoption, vocational training/job development and other important services for the African-American community.

***Chicago Race Riot 1919***
*(Illinois Institute of Technology Campus)*
*CTA station 35th & State St.*
*Bronzeville*

Chicago Police Officer, John Simpson, was killed here. An effort has been started to name the new Chicago Police Central Headquarters in honor of Officer Simpson

Although Lake Michigan forms the eastern border of Bronzeville, tension between blacks and whites pervaded the area. On July 27, 1919, an African-American youth was swimming at the 29th Street beach when a rock-throwing fight ensued. Because of the danger on shore, the youth, Eugene Williams, drowned when he could no longer hold on to a railroad tie. Although the coroner's inquest listed the cause of death as drowning, it was believed that the boy was stoned to death. Five days of rioting ensued, during which, 23 blacks and 15 whites, were killed, and hundreds were wounded. A lengthy coroner's report was produced, which gave recommendations to the city about how to deal with the problem of racism and tension between the races.

*Pilgrim Baptist Church—built in 1890-91*
*3301 S. Indiana*

As was the case with many African-American churches in Chicago and elsewhere, Pilgrim Baptist Church progressed from a devoted prayer group to a dynamic congregation. The Union Grove Prayer Meeting Club met in the years of World War I and soon became Pilgrim Baptist Church under the leadership of its first pastor, Reverend J.D. Luck of New York. During the years the church experienced ministerial difficulties and misunderstandings, but renewed its mission during the 1920s when Dr. S.E. Watson became the spiritual leader. During this period the church attracted many new members and through the efforts of many of the faithful, Pilgrim was able to purchase and occupy its current site in 1921, which they purchased from the Jewish community. Designed by Louis Sullivan, the famous Chicago architect who created the Auditorium Theater and the Chicago Board of Trade Building, the church is decorated inside and outside with ornamentation and imaginative designs. It is regarded as a marvelous example of ecclesiastical architecture. In the façade above the front entrance there is a Hebrew inscription and also an English one: "Open the gates of righteousness, that I may enter thru them."

Today, Pilgrim Baptist has a church school, a community center, and a new administration center. It has been designated a Chicago landmark.

*Unity Hall*
*3140 S. Indiana*

Renamed in 1917, Unity Hall was originally a Jewish social club. It became the headquarters of the Peoples' Movement, a political organization led by Congressman Oscar DePriest (1871-1951). Born in Florence Alabama, Oscar DePriest was the first African-American congressman of the 20th Century. He was the first African American to serve in the City Council. DePriest became 2nd Ward alderman in 1915, Cook County commissioner, and was a three-time delegate to the Republican National Convention.

L.B. Dixon, a local architect noted for designing many residences in the area, designed Unity Hall. The building is faced in red pressed brick, with terra cotta and sheet metal trim. Its interior included small clubrooms in front and a large assembly hall in the rear

**Olivet Baptist Church**
*3101 S. King Drive (Formerly known as South Park)*

Chicago's oldest African-American Baptist congregation, Olivet Baptist was originally organized as Zenia Baptist Church in 1850. The church experienced tremendous growth through the years and moved from time to time to accommodate the size of the congregation. Dr. Lacey Williams became the pastor of Olivet in 1916. Under his leadership, Olivet became the largest African-American and the largest Protestant church in the world. In addition to his pastorate at Olivet, where many programs were developed to help the congregation and the community, such as a nursery school, a home for working girls, and a kindergarten, Dr. Williams served as the president of the National Baptist Convention.

Several other pastors have helped Olivet maintain its tradition of national and international prominence begun by Dr. Williams. In 1992 Dr. Michael Noble became pastor. With determination and with the help of God, Olivet has endured periods of unrest and dissention over the leadership of the church and remains one of the strong congregations in the Bronzeville community.

*Griffin Funeral Home*—*Site of Camp Douglas*
*Civil War Training and Induction Center*
*3232 S. King Drive*

During the Civil War, a Union Army training post was built at 31st Street between Cottage Grove and South Parkway. It served as a Confederate prisoner of war camp from 1862-1865, housing approximately 26,000 Confederate soldiers in temporary, wooden barracks. Because of the harsh conditions, approximately four thousand men died and were buried in unmarked pauper's graves in the Chicago City Cemetery, located in what is now the southeast corner of Lincoln Park.

Because of the unsanitary conditions of the shallow graves, which were dug in marshy land, health officials urged that the graves be moved. Also, wealthy residents living on Astor Street, Dearborn Parkway, and Lake Shore Drive wanted a park to be constructed for their enjoyment. The remains were relocated in 1866 to Oak Woods Cemetery on the south side and to Rose Hill Cemetery on the north side.

Two of the more famous prisoners at Camp Douglas were Sam Houston, Jr., governor of Texas who was removed from office because he opposed secession from the Union, and Henry M. Stanley, African explorer (of "Dr. Livingston, I presume" fame).

*Roloson Houses—Erected 1894*
*3213-19 South Calumet*

Dedicated as a Chicago landmark in 1979, the Roloson Houses were designed by Frank Lloyd Wright. Famous for his

Prairie School of Architecture houses, Wright designed the rowhouses as an investment property for Robert W. Roloson, a wealthy grain merchant. The façades had deeply pitched triangle bands and rectangular windows in English Tudor style. There was terra cotta ornament decorating the face between the second and third floors. This decoration was from the influence of Louis Sullivan, who was the mentor of Wright.

**Douglas Academy**
*3200 S. Calumet*

**Engine Company 19**
*3421 S. Calumet*

One of the earlier fire engine companies organized with black fireman. Mayor Joseph Medill appointed the first African-American fireman to lieutenant in 1871.

***Victory Monument***
*Honors Black soldiers of Illinois who served in World War I*

This monument was erected at 35th and King Drive to honor the soldiers of the Eighth Regiment of the Illinois National Guard. This African-American unit served valiantly in France during World War I.

Leonard Crunelle, a protégé of the famous Chicago sculptor, Lorado Taft, sculpted the soldier figure and the bronze panels. The monument was dedicated in 1928 on Armistice Day (November 11).

***Home of***
***Etta Moten Barnett***
*3619 S. King Drive*

A very special entertainer, Etta Moten Barnett was a singer

and actress who received several honors during her career. She was invited to sing in the White House for Franklin and Eleanor Roosevelt. She was also invited by Gershwin himself to play the part of Bess in Porgy and Bess. In addition to her show business career, Barnett was also a successful lecturer, civic and community worker, arts patron, and African-affairs specialist. Well known for a voice that "cut through like a trumpet", Barnett starred in several Broadway and touring musicals and she sang in films such as Flying Down to Rio, which starred Fred Astaire and Ginger Rogers.

*Home of Ida B. Wells Barnett*
*3624 S. King Drive*

Ida B. Wells was the most successful and most famous black female journalist in the country in her day. In her newspaper, Free Speech, she detailed the racial injustices that blacks endured in Memphis, Tennessee. After her story appeared describing the lynching of three black prisoners, a mob broke into Wells' newspaper offices and destroyed the printing equipment and all the copies of the newspaper they could find. Ms. Wells continued to publicize the facts of lynching while working for the New York Age. She led an appeal to President William McKinley for support in fighting this horrible practice. A native of Mississippi, Wells came to Chicago and married a newspaper journalist, Ferdinand Barnett in 1895. They worked together fighting injustice. Wells was one of the original organizers of the national conference out of which grew the N.A.A.C.P (National Association for the Advancement of Colored People).

The home incorporates elements of the Romanesque-revival and Queen Anne styles of architecture.

*Home of Dr. George Cleveland Hall* *(1864-1930)*
*3638 S. King Drive*

Dr. Hall helped Dr. Daniel Hale Williams to organize Provident Hospital in 1890 where he served as surgeon-in-chief. As one of the leading physicians in Chicago for many years, Hall founded the Cook County Physicians Association. As a fighter for the rights of African Americans, Hall worked with the Chicago Urban League, became an active member of the NAACP, and helped to found the Association for the Study of Negro Life and History. The Hall Branch Library at 48th and Michigan was named after Dr. Hall, who was the second African-American to serve on the board of the Chicago Public Library.

*Home of Lu Palmer*
*CBUC/BIPO Headquarters*
*on 37th St.*
*3656 S. King Drive*

Lutrell "Lu" Palmer is a community activist and organizer long known as a journalist with the Chicago Defender and the Daily News. He was added to the list of the influential black journalists of the 20th Century.

*Eighth Regiment Armory*
*3517-33 S. Giles*

Now the Chicago Military Academy, Bronzeville a Chicago Public High School, this was the first armory built in the United States for soldiers in an African-American regiment. The "Fighting 8th" as it came to be known developed from a volunteer militia called the Hannibal Guard in 1871. Later it was a part of the Illinois National Guard during World War I and was incorporated into the 370th U.S. Infantry. The armory was closed in the early 1960s, but was used as the South Central Gymnasium. The Chicago Board of Education acquired the site and began an extensive renovation to make it into a high school with a military twist.

James B. Dibelka, a Chicagoan and chief architect of the State of Illinois designed this impressive building. Its façade is brown pressed brick and Bedford limestone.

Joseph Thompson, a retired Chicago Policeman, recalls his youth while living at 35th and Giles. Mr.Thompson describes some of the unique characters that would come by to entertain the residents. They included the organ grinder and monkey that would perform. He also tells the story of the man who would come around with a bear on a metal chain. The most interesting character was K.C. Jones, who was known as chicken man. He would bring four or five chickens in a burlap sack or croker and the chickens would do tricks, but the chicken man would always say: "no dime, no show."

Soldiers from the 8th Regiment would burn their old uniforms and clothing in a vacant lot next to the Armory once a year. Before setting fire to a huge pile of clothing, the soldiers would allow the people who needed clothing to come over and take what they needed.

*Douglas Tomb State Memorial*
*35th and Cottage Grove Ave.*

Designated as a Chicago Landmark in 1977, Douglas Tomb honors Stephen A. Douglas, United States Senator from Illinois. Douglas died in 1861. He is famous for the debates with Abraham Lincoln over the issue of slavery during their campaign for the U.S. presidency. He was also a very important character in the development of Chicago. As an early investor in Chicago real estate, the tomb stands on land that was once part of his 53-acre estate, Oakenwald. A street in the neighborhood bears that name today. The architect of the tomb was Leonard Volk, who is also famous for casting the face and hands of Abraham Lincoln, which were used by Augustus St. Gaudens to create the standing Lincoln statue in Lincoln Park.

# Black Metropolis Thematic District

Officially designated as the Black Metropolis Thematic District was the area from the intersection of 35th and State Street. There were eight buildings and one monument which comprised the District:

1. Overton Hygenic Building/Douglas National Bank
2. Chicago Bee Building
3. Wabash Avenue YMCA
4. Chicago Defender Building (early location at 3435 S. Indiana)
5. Unity Hall
6. Eighth Regiment Armory
7. Sunset Café/Terrace Café (at 315 E. 35th Street
8. Victory Monument
9. Supreme Life Insurance Building (at 35th and King Drive).

*(See Map on page 51)*

*Overton Hygenic Building and Douglas National Bank*
*3619-27 S. State Street*

Anthony Overton was one of the most influential entrepreneurs of the early 20th Century. This four-story building housed the Overton cosmetics business as well as other black-owned businesses in the Black Metropolis, the community we call Bronzeville. This community developed in response to the restrictions and exploitation blacks experienced in Chicago in the early 1900s. Overton was recognized for his accomplishments by the NAACP, which rewarded him with the Spingarn Medal, the only one ever awarded for business. He also won the Harmon Award for business in 1927.

Douglass National Bank was the first national bank founded, owned and controlled by African Americans. Under Overton's leadership, the bank achieved a high level of success throughout the 1920s and 1930s. Following the county, state and federal government, Chicago began a series of deposits, which amounted to $30,000 in 1933. As the Chicago Defender wrote, "the first national bank in the country run and owned by the Race."

*Chicago Bee Building*
*3647 S. State Street*

Built a few years after the Overton Hygenic Building, 1929-31, the Chicago Bee Building housed the Chicago Bee newspaper, which was published by Anthony Overton. The newspaper was very important to the Black Metropolis for its news articles and advertisements relevant to the black community. It is reported that the term Bronzeville came about as a term used and popularized by one of the editors of the newspaper. The newspaper was published into the 1940s and eventually went out of business.

Overton wanted the building to be a structure of high quality and beauty and for that reason he hired a well-known South Side architect named Z. Eroi Smith, who designed the building in the art deco style of the day.

The Chicago Bee Building has been completely restored and currently houses a Chicago Public Library Branch, which opened in 1996. It also houses a Family Literacy Center on the second floor, which is sponsored by the DePaul University and the Chicago Public Library.

Quote from a 1929 ad for the Chicago Bee Newspaper:

What the Bee stands for:

*"The suppression of superstition—with enlightenment. Higher education for all groups. Cordial relation between the races. Civic and racial improvement and development. The promotion of Negro business. Good, wholesome and authentic news for any member of the family."*

**Wabash Avenue YMCA**
*3763 S. Wabash Avenue*

Opened in 1913, the Wabash Avenue YMCA became a center for education and culture in the Black Metropolis. Its architect was Robert C. Berlin. Funding for the construction came from Julius Rosenwald, chairman of Sears, Roebuck and Company. Rosenwald was a generous philanthropist who was very intent upon improving the life and welfare of black people. He was instrumental in helping to construct YMCAs in other cities with the help of community support. The YMCA became a center for the assistance of the many blacks who migrated to Chicago from the south between 1915 and 1920. It offered educational classes and job training and helped people to find housing. Carter G. Woodson founded the Association for the Study of Negro life and Culture there in 1915

The Wabash Avenue YMCA was dedicated a Chicago Landmark in 1998.

**Augustus Lewis Williams**
3646 S. Michigan Ave.

Represented families of African Americans who were killed or injured during the 1919 Chicago Race riots

**Dr. Margaret Goss Burroughs Home**
Founder of the DuSable Museum of African
American History
**John W. Griffiths Mansion**
3806 S. Michigan Avenue

*DuSable Museum*
*of African American History*

Dr. Margaret Burroughs is the principal founder of the DuSable Museum of African-American History. She started the museum in her home and now it is one of the foremost American institutions preserving the culture and history of African Americans. Dr. Burroughs studied art at the School of the Art Institute of Chicago. She also taught art at DuSable High School for 23 years. She is known the world over for her paintings and also for her writing. In addition to writing children's books, she has written several books of poetry. The poem "What Shall I Tell My Children Who Are Black?" is read all over the world.

*South Side Community Arts Center* Built in 1892-93
3831 S. Michigan Avenue

The South Side Community Arts Center opened in

December 1941 as an institution for the African-American community where artists could develop and display their talents and provide inspiration and education to young aspiring artists. The original staff was supported by the federal Works Progress Administration (WPA) and Eleanor Roosevelt was present for the dedication. After the WPA funding ended, the Center has supported itself with memberships and contributions from the African-American community.

Over the years the Center has presented over 450 art exhibits. Artists who have been associated with the Center include noted sculptor, Richard Hunt and photojournalist Gordon Parks. Other artists who have been involved include Gwendolyn Brooks, the Pulitzer-Prize-winning poet; Margaret Burroughs, founder of the DuSable Museum of African-American History; Etta Moten Barnett, singer, actress, and community leader, artist Archibald Motley, and many more.

The South Side Community Arts Center was the proud winner of the Governor's Award for the Arts in 1982.

This Georgian revival-style residence was built in 1892-93 for grain merchant George Seaverns, Jr. It was remodeled in 1940 for use by the Center. Its interior is an example of New Bauhaus-style design. It was designated a Chicago Landmark in 1994.

*CYC-Elliott Donnelley Center*
*3947 S. Michigan*

One of the oldest social service agencies in Chicago, the

Elliott Donnelley Youth Center was originally established as the South Side Boys Club in 1924. The mission of the Center is to serve children in the community with programs to help them to reach their full potential. Each year approximately 1,500 youth participate in center-based programs, school collaborations, and special projects. Programs focus on developing youth leadership and drug prevention. There is an after-school program that includes tutorial/homework assistance, a recreation and sports programs, computer training, and much more.

***St. Elizabeth's Catholic Church***
4058 S. Michigan

Chicago's first African-American Catholic Priest to preside over a congregation

Originally founded by an Irish priest, the Rev. Daniel J. Riordan, St. Elizabeth Parish has a long history of providing spiritual and educational assistance to its parishioners, students, and to the neighboring community. St. Elizabeth merged with St. Monica in 1921, a parish that was founded by the first black priest in the U.S., Father John AugustineTolton. St. Elizabeth also opened the first black Catholic high school in Chicago in 1926.

The parish continues to be very active within the community, working with other churches and community institutions to provide housing, job training, and after-school programs for neighborhood children.

**First Church of Deliverance** *Built in 1939*
*4315 S. Wabash Avenue*

Designed by the first African-American architect in Chicago, Walter T. Bailey, First Church of Deliverance is a unique church in style and substance. The Art Moderne style is characterized by a terra cotta façade and twin towers. Founded by Reverend Clarence H. Cobbs, First Church of Deliverance has played an important role in Christian radio broadcasting and the development of gospel music.

**8th Church of Christ Scientist** *Built in 1910-11*
*4359 S. Michigan Avenue*

This classical-style church houses the oldest African-

American Christian Science congregation in the country. The classical-revival style of the building was made famous at the 1893 World's Columbian Exposition, the extremely popular world's fair in Chicago's Jackson Park. The church features a temple front and a broad dome. The 8th Church of Christ, Scientist was designed by architect Leon E. Stanhope. It was designated a Chicago landmark in 1993.

*Chicago Urban League*
*4510 S. Michigan Avenue*

The Chicago Urban League was organized in 1916 to combat racial discrimination and segregation in housing in Chicago. It continues to fight for equal opportunities for African-Americans, other minorities and the poor in every aspect of life in America. The Chicago Urban League has programs to educate the citizens in the Bronzeville community and has opened a learning center complete with a computer lab. The League also focused on economic progress and empowerment for the community.

*Swift Mansion*
*4500 South Michigan Avenue*

Built just prior to the World's Columbian Exposition of 1893, the Swift House was one of many large and exquisite dwellings built along Chicago's major avenues and boulevards. Mr. and Mrs. Edward Morris originally owned the mansion. Morris was president of one of the world's leading meatpacking companies, Morris and Company, which was only rivaled in size by Armour and Swift, also located in Chicago. Mrs. Morris was the daughter of Gustavus Swift, who founded Swift and Company. The architectural style of the mansion is similar to the style of H.H. Richardson, a famous artist of the day. It features a great stone exterior along with large curved castle-like cylindrical forms. As with many such dwellings of the day, the interior features large parlors, an elegant stairwell leading to the second and third floors, and extensive woodwork.

At one point the mansion housed the social service program of the Chicago Urban League. It is currently owned by Inner City Youth Foundation and is home to several human services and cultural programs. Swift House was designated a landmark on the National Register of Historic Places in 1968 and as an Illinois Historic Structure in 1972

# A View of Bronzeville

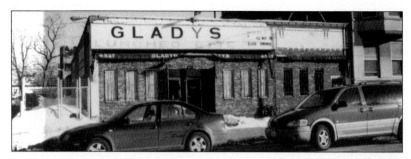

***Glady's Luncheonette***
4527 S. Indiana

The Great Migration brought many to Chicago, who were looking for a better life. One of Chicago's longest-lasting eating establishments was opened by Gladys Joyner Holcombe, who came to Chicago around 1945 from Memphis, where she had been a waitress at the Greyhound Bus Station. The original Glady's Luncheonette was at 4541 S. Indiana. Gladys was the cook and her husband served the food. Filling a need for handy, delicious, home-style cooking, the luncheonette grew and eventually relocated to 4527 Indiana, its current location. The tradition continues and people from the community and beyond can still get soul food such as biscuits, fried and smothered pork chops, ribs, chittlins, greens, macaroni and cheese, and fried cabbage.

***Michigan Boulevard Garden Apartments***
*47th Street and Michigan Avenue*

The population of African-Americans in Chicago during the years between 1910 and 1930 grew from 44,000 to 234,000. Although the population increased, the boundaries of the "Black Belt" remained the same due to the restrictive covenants in place that did not allow blacks to move into other parts of the city. Julius Rosenwald, one of the foremost philanthropists of the time (and Chairman of Sears, Roebuck & Co.) wanted to build some affordable, safe, and clean housing for African Americans. He purchased six acres of land between 46th and 47th streets and Michigan and Wabash Avenues for the Michigan Boulevard Garden Apartments. Completed in 1929 at a cost of $2.7 Million, the Michigan Boulevard Garden Apartments contained 421 units in five-story-light-brick-walkup buildings. There is a huge interior courtyard that is accessed by eight terra cotta doorways from the street. The building also contained 14 stores.

The architect was Ernest Grusfield, Jr., who later designed the Adler Planetarium. As expected, there was much criticism of this private initiative to create public low-cost housing for blacks, however, Rosenwald was successful in completing the project. Unfortunately, with the onslaught of the depression, people were not able to pay the rents and the project was a financial disaster. Rosenwald died in 1932.

*Gerri's Palm Tavern*
*446 E. 47th St.*

Gerri's Palm tavern is the last and most authentic remnant of historic Bronzeville. Located on 47th Street in the heart of what was a vibrant community, where businesses flourished, people shopped and worked by day and partied the night away, Gerri's opened its doors in 1933. The Chicago Defender called it "the most high classed Negro establishment in America."

The Palm Tavern played a huge role in the development of jazz and blues music and was patronized the royalty of the Negro music world. Regal Theater performers such as Duke Ellington, Count Basie, Muddy Waters, Quincy Jones and James Brown as well as many others visited Gerri's for food, drinks, and conversation.

The Palm Tavern was originally opened as a restaurant by James "Genial Jim" Knight, the first Mayor of Bronzeville, in May, 1933. He managed the Palm Tavern until 1956. Genial Jim sold it to Gerri "Mama Gerri" Oliver, who the tavern ever since. The Palm was an important part of history and should have been an important part of the planned revitalization of the area.

# Bronzeville and The Mayor of Bronzeville

Bronzeville got its name from James "Jimmy" Gentry, a Chicago Defender writer and club promoter. Jimmy Gentry was instrumental in promoting the Miss Bronze America beauty pageants. His idea was that the Mayor of Bronzeville would be an individual who would lead and represent the community and speak up on issues that affected the people of the area. People began to like the idea and enthusiastically supported several candidates by voting at the local business establish-ments, churches and news-stands. On Saturday, September 22, 1934, Genial Jim Knight was elected the first-ever Mayor of Bronzeville. Although the Mayor was not an official of gov-ernment or sanctioned by a political party, he was respected and recog-nized by African Americans in Bronzeville. Among those who have had the honor to serve include two successful physicians and a top radio personality, Herb Kent.

*Herb Kent.*

# A View of Bronzeville

**George C. Hall Branch Library**

**First Public Library built in the African-American Community**
*4801 S. Michigan Ave.*

Named after the well-known surgeon George C. Hall, the library was a center for literary discussions in the 1930s and 1940s. Authors such as Arna Bontemps, Zora Neal Hurston, Claude McKay, Langston Hughes, and Richard Wright met at the Hall Branch Library. It was first opened in 1932 under the direction of the first African-American librarian in Chicago, Vivian Harsh.

Another important figure in the field of children's literature worked at the library from 1932-1963. Charlamae Hill Rollins was children's librarian, author and storyteller, who served as the first African-American president of the children's services division of the American Library Association.

**Harold Washington,** Chicago's first African American mayor, lived across the street at 4736 S. Michigan as a child.

**Oscar S. DePriest Home**
*4536-38 S. King Drive*

Born in Florence, Alabama in 1871, Oscar B. DePriest was the first African American elected to Congress in the 21st Century. Prior to serving as U.S. congressman, DePriest was the first African American elected to the Chicago City Council from the Second Ward. He served in several other positions, including Cook County Commissioner. He was also a three-time delegate to the Republican National Convention. After his defeat for Congress in 1934, he became a real estate broker. He served as alderman again from 1943-1947.

**Mt. Pisgah Missionary Baptist Church**
*4622 S. King Drive*

Reverend G.W. Alexander and several other founding members founded another of Bronzeville's important houses of worship, Mt. Pisgah, in 1926. According to the church's history, a repenting sinner was baptized on the occasion of the first meeting. The church had several homes in the ensuing years and continued to grow. Recognizing the poverty and hopelessness in the surrounding community during the years after the depression, the church, under the leadership of Reverend Joseph Wells, encouraged people in the community to rebuild homes and businesses, as well as their spiritual lives.

The current church edifice was dedicated in October 1962, after much work and effort by the pastor and congregation. Mt. Pisgah worked with Dr. Martin Luther King in his struggle for civil rights during the 1960s and eventually built the Dr. Martin Luther King Jr. Urban Progress Center, which provides employment, health, and recreation services to improve the community. It currently houses the Firman Community Service & New Day Youth Project and thrives as a congregation that seeks to better the community.

*Robert Abbott Home*
*4742 S. King Drive*

Founder of the Chicago Defender, Robert Sengstacke migrated to Chicago from Georgia. He earned a law degree from Kent College of Law but because of racial discrimination was unable to practice. The Defender became the widest-circulated black newspaper in the country.

*Fact:*

Cottage Grove Avenue was originally an old Indian trail. Because the path was widely used, city planners paved roads on its course.

**Operation PUSH Headquarters,** *founder Jesse L. Jackson*
*930 E. 50th Street*

Founded in 1971 by Jesse Jackson, Operation PUSH (People United to Save Humanity) sought to promote economic progress for African-American people and businesses and to assist African-American urban youth. The organization has continued to be a leader in causes such as promoting educational improvement, minority employment, and national politics.

Today, this edifice is the national headquarters of The Rainbow/PUSH Coalition, also founded by Jackson to continue the work started by Operation PUSH. Its efforts include people of diverse ethnic, religious, political, and economic backgrounds. The goal is to gain access to capital, economic equity, and empowerment for all people.

***Drexel Kenwood Mansion***
*4801 S. Drexel Blvd.*

**Julius Rosenwald Home**
*4901 S. Ellis Avenue*

Rosenwald was a successful retail manager who gained notoriety when he was asked to become vice-president of Sears, Roebuck & Company when it moved to Chicago in 1893. He subsequently served as president and chairman of the board of Sears until 1932. He is credited with creating the concept of mail-order sales and created one of the first savings and profit-sharing plans for employees. Rosenwald is well-known for his philanthropy, having provided funds for schools for African-Americans in rural areas and low-cost housing for African-Americans in Chicago. He also provided funding for YMCA and YWCA buildings in programs all around the country.

***Provident Hospital***—*Original Site opened in 1891*
*500 E. 51st St.*

Because there was no access to nursing education for African-American women nor hospital privileges for African-American physicians, Dr. Daniel Hale Williams, with the support of Chicago ministers, physicians, and businessmen, decided to found a nursing school for black women. Support and assistance for this project came from wealthy white citizens such as Phillip Danforth Armour, Marshall Field, and George Pullman, as well as black businessmen, organizations, and individual donors. Provident Hospital's first home was a former meatpacking house at 29th and Dearborn. It originally had twelve beds in a three-story facility. Later, the hospital moved to a larger facility, a sixty-five bed building at 36th and Dearborn.

Dr. Daniel Hale Williams is credited with being the first to perform open-heart surgery. Under his leadership and the board of trustees, Provident continued to be a fine medical institution for the African American community, although there was controversy about whether the institution should have chosen several notable white physicians, such as Frank Billings and Christian Fenger, over African-American physicians. Provident relocated to 51st and Vincennes in 1929 and eventually became an affiliate of Cook County Hospital in 1974. The new facility opened in 1992.

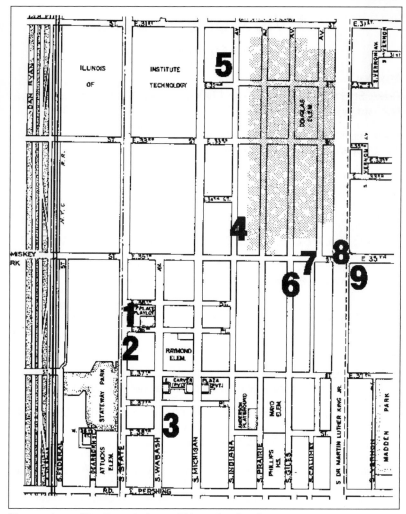

Map courtesy of the Commission on Chicago Landmarks

1. Overton Hygenic Building/Douglas National Bank
2. Chicago Bee Building
3. Wabash Avenue YMCA
4. Chicago Defender Building (early location at 3435 S. Indiana)
5. Unity Hall
6. Eighth Regiment Armory
7. Sunset Café/Terrace Café (at 315 E. 35th Street
8. Victory Monument
9. Supreme Life Insurance Building (at 35th and King Drive).

# A View of Bronzeville
# Bibliography

## Books

Drake, St. Clair and Horace Cayton. Black Metropolis: A Study of Negro Life in a Northern City. New York: Harcourt Brace & World, Inc. 1970, 1972, 1945

Spear, Allan H. Black Chicago The Making of a Negro Ghetto 1890-1920. Chicago: The University of Chicago Press. 1967

Lehman, Nicholas; The Promise Land. New York; Knopf

Ottley, Roi. The Lonely Warrior: The Life and Times of Robert S. Abbott. Chicago: H. Regnery Co., 1955

Sandburg, Carl. The Chicago Race Riots. New York: Harcourt, Brace & World, Inc. 1919

Adams, Rosemary K. A Wild Kind of Boldness The Chicago History Reader. Chicago: Wm. B. Eerdmans Publishing Co. Chicago Historical Society

Williams, Sherry. Bronzeville/Black Chicago 100 Notable People and Places. Chicago. 1999

## Resources

Chicago's Black Metropolis—Reading Collection Vivian Harsh. Woodson Regional Library Samuelson, Timothy "Black Metropolis Thematic Nomination, 1986

"To Die in Chicago: Confederate Prisoners at Camp Douglas, 1862-1865. 1994. Levy, George. Evanston: Evanston Publishing Co. Guide to Public Art in Bronzeville. Chicago Department of Cultural Affairs. 1996

"Provident Hospital: America's First Free Standing Black Hospital" Chicago Defender

"Palm holds both history and her story" Dawn Turner Trice Chicago Tribune; 2001

Black Metropolis Historic District. Submitted to the Commission On Chicago Landmarks on March 7, 1984

Chicago Historical Society

Notable Black American Women

Notable Black American Men

DuSable Museum of African American History Newsletter/Calendar of Events, October, November, December 2000

# A View of Bronzeville
# Index

# *NOTES*